torical Eras

An Interactive History Adventure

by Terry Collins

Consultant:
Hanchao Lu, PhD, Professor
School of History, Technology & Society
Georgia Institute of Technology

CAPSTONE PRESS
a capstone imprint

You Choose Books are published by Capstone Press,
1710 Roe Crest Drive, North Mankato, Minnesota 56003.
www.capstonepub.com

Library of Congress Cataloging-in-Publication Data
Collins, Terry
 Ancient China : an interactive history adventure / by Terry Collins.
   p. cm. — (You choose books. Historical eras)
 Includes bibliographical references and index.
 Summary: "Describes the life and times of the era known as ancient China. The readers' choices
reveal the historical details of life during the Qin dynasty, life under Empress Wu Zetian, and life
as a trader on the Silk Road"—Provided by publisher.
 ISBN 978-1-4296-4778-6 (library binding)
 ISBN 978-1-4296-9472-8 (paperback)
 ISBN 978-1-62065-376-0 (ebook PDF)
 1. China—Civilization—To 221 B.C.—Juvenile literature. 2. China—Civilization—
221 B.C.–960 A.D.—Juvenile literature. I. Title.
 DS741.65.C645 2013
 931—dc23   2012006809

Editorial Credits
Kristen Mohn, editor; Bobbie Nuytten, designer; Wanda Winch, media researcher;
    Danielle Ceminsky, production specialist

Photo Credits
Alamy: Interfoto, 9, North Wind Picture Archives: 72, TAO Images Limited/Zhang Shuo,
100, View Stock, 44; Art Resource, N.Y.: Eileen Tweedy, 57; The Bridgeman Art Library
International/Bibliotheque Nationale, Paris, France, 14, Private Collection/ Komi Chen, 69,
© Look and Learn/Private Collection/James Edwin McConnell, 102, © Look and Learn/
Private Collection/Pat Nicolle, 43, Peter Newark Pictures/Private Collection, 91, The Stapleton
Collection/Private Collection/H.M. Burton, 38; © Caroline Young, All Rights Reserved,
49; Corbis: National Geographic Society/Hsien-Min Yang, cover, 35, Wolfgang Kaehler, 79;
Courtesy of SACU-Society for Anglo Chinese Understanding, 26; Dreamstime: Anhong, 96;
The Granger Collection, NYC, 85; Osprey Publishing: "The Great Wall of China 221 BC-AD
1644", Steve Noon, artist, 21; Shutterstock: Feng Yu, 61; SuperStock, Inc: SuperStock, 82

Printed in the United States of America in Brainerd, Minnesota.
032012   006672BANGF12

TABLE OF CONTENTS

ABOUT YOUR ADVENTURE

YOU are living in the vast country of ancient China. It's an exciting time of many new discoveries and inventions. It's also a time of many rules and laws, according to the emperor in power. It's not always easy to follow these laws. Will you be able to please the emperor?

In this book you'll explore how the choices people made meant the difference between life and death. The events you'll experience happened to real people.

Chapter One sets the scene. Then you choose which path to read. Follow the directions at the bottom of each page. The choices you make will change your outcome. After you finish your path, go back and read the others for new perspectives and more adventures.

YOU CHOOSE the path
you take through history.

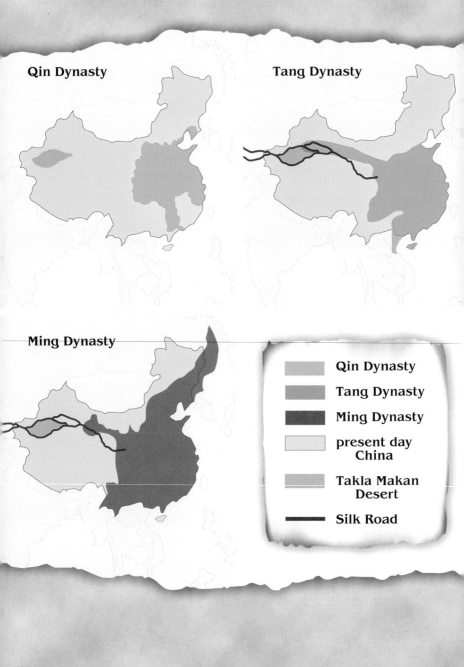

Qin Dynasty

Tang Dynasty

Ming Dynasty

	Qin Dynasty
	Tang Dynasty
	Ming Dynasty
	present day China
	Takla Makan Desert
	Silk Road

Ancient Leaders, Ancient Dynasties

China is home to one of the oldest civilizations in the world. Its culture is a rich one, filled with philosophy, science, and invention.

The time period known as ancient China began about 4000 years ago. Much of this time in China's history was ruled by dynasties. A dynasty is a ruling family and the period of time they are in power. Some dynasties lasted for hundreds of years, while others lasted fewer than 20 years. Each dynasty had unique qualities. Each ruler brought in new ideas and customs.

Turn the page.

Historians believe the first dynasty, the Xia Dynasty, began as far back as 2000 BC. Early dynasties such as Xia were led by kings or rulers.

Around 200 BC the Qin Dynasty brought the first emperor to power—Qin Shi Huangdi. He oversaw the joining of China from seven major states into one mighty country. He built roads and canals, issued the same kind of money for all, and demanded that one written language be used.

But Qin Shi Huangdi could be cruel. He came up with a set of strict laws. Later dynasties changed some of them, but one concept remained the same. Ancient Chinese people believed the emperor was sent from heaven to rule. To defy the emperor could mean punishment, imprisonment, or death.

Qin Shi Huangdi called himself the first emperor of China.

9

Turn the page.

Two philosophers developed ideas that shaped the way ancient Chinese people lived. Around 600 BC Laozi founded the philosophy of Taoism. Taoism said that people should live in harmony with the universe. They should also work with nature for an easy life.

Soon after Laozi came another philosopher known as Confucius. He believed if people respected and followed the teachings of their elders and superiors, all would be good. The teachings of Confucius were not appreciated in his lifetime. But after his death, his ideas helped form a basis for Chinese government for thousands of years.

During the dynasties' rule, society became more structured. The intellectual class could read and write. They helped govern all of China under the emperor. Many of these men became public servants, working as judges and tax collectors after passing a test. Women were rarely allowed to work as public servants. Their education was generally limited to homemaking skills.

Peasants were below the intellectual class in the social order. Land was taken from rich noblemen and shared among the peasants to farm. Peasants grew food for the army and the people who lived in cities. Peasants were very poor, but also important to China's well being.

Turn the page.

Next were the artisans. These skilled workers made weapons, pottery, tools, and other useful items. Many artisans passed on their skills to their children, creating long family lines of creative and skilled craftsmen.

The merchants were the lowest rung on the social ladder. Since merchants only bought and sold goods, society viewed them as unworthy. Despite their social standing, merchants often were the wealthiest people in China.

Apart from all of these classes was the professional soldier. To be a part of China's army was not a great honor. Common infantrymen were considered an even lower class than the merchants. Some generals became career military men. But most army members were drafted, or called upon to serve, for two years.

There is no single date considered to be the end of the ancient Chinese era. But many historians believe it ended in 1911 with the fall of the last dynasty, the Qing Dynasty.

Today China is a blend of ideas and customs from many dynasties. China has become one of the most powerful nations in the world. Knowing its past is necessary to understanding this unique country.

➤To explore life in China under Emperor Qin in 213 BC, turn to page **15**.

➤To help a man on the run in AD 691 during the rule of Empress Wu Zetian, turn to page **45**.

➤To travel the dangerous pathways of the Silk Road during the Ming Dynasty in 1420, turn to page **73**.

Emperor Qin restricted the study of books.

CHAPTER 2

Scholar or Soldier?

The year is 213 BC, during the time of the Qin Dynasty. Emperor Qin Shi Huangdi's vision of a country united under a single ruler has come true. Thanks to the strength of his army, the seven major kingdoms of China are now joined as one.

You are the 16-year-old son of one of the emperor's most trusted generals, Qi Kong. You are well trained by your father in the military arts He hopes that you will follow him into the military. You are also well educated. Your love of books and history sometimes puts you at odds with your father. He is concerned about your thirst for knowledge.

15

Turn the page.

Acting on the advice of Li Si, his chief adviser, the emperor has banned many books. One banned book, the *Analects*, collects the lessons of Confucius as written by his students. Confucius said that a ruler had to respect his subjects, just as his subjects must respect him.

Confucius' teachings differ greatly from the emperor's ideas. The emperor believes in a system called legalism, which requires strict discipline and laws. Under legalism, an emperor's word is law. Failure to destroy forbidden books brings great punishment, including death.

A lighter punishment might be forced labor on the building of the Great Wall. This wall was Emperor Qin's attempt to protect the northern border of China from invading armies. It would eventually stretch more than 5,000 miles.

You find yourself torn between the way of the warrior and the path of the scholar. While you believe your father to be a great man, you wonder if the life of a soldier is for you.

→To become a soldier like your father, turn to page **18**.

→To become a scholar, turn to page **19**.

Early one morning you awaken to find Qi Kong standing by your bedside in his uniform. He's covered in tough body armor. His hat looks like a bird. It symbolizes his bravery and skill.

"My son, our most wise and gracious emperor has asked me to inspect the building of the Great Wall to the north. Would you like to go with me?"

"Yes!" you reply eagerly, but then you remember. "Oh, wait. I have school."

"Ah," your father says with a tone of disapproval. "Well, do you wish to go on an adventure or stay and continue your studies?" You sense the unspoken challenge in his voice. Your father wants you to focus on the life of a soldier and is ready for your schooling to end.

➤ To go with Qi Kong to see the Great Wall, turn to page **20**.

➤ To stay home, turn to page **23**.

18

You sit comfortably in your bedroom and read the words of the emperor. The stories of his wisdom are well known to you. With your keen imagination, you feel as if you were there at his side.

You also know earlier history books were all destroyed by royal order. You are sure the emperor had his reasons, but wonder what those books said that required them to be burned. You have asked your teachers, but they tell you to be silent. To speak of such books is forbidden.

One morning, your curiosity is rewarded. There is a note tucked under your seating mat at school. "For the scholar in search of the old scrolls, meet me at dusk in the garden behind the library."

➤To go to the meeting, turn to page **24**.

➤To show the note to your father, turn to page **30**.

You leap to your feet. "It would be an honor to see the Great Wall!"

Qi Kong grunts. "Then gather your things and join me outside."

As you walk through the front door, the cool morning air welcomes you. "Why does the emperor wish such a great wall to be built, Father?" you ask.

He smiles. "For protection from our enemies to the north. Nearly eight years ago, 30,000 men were sent to begin work on the wall."

"To be given such a task from the emperor must be a great honor," you say.

Your father laughs. "Honor? Hah! Most of the builders are simple peasants. There are also convicts working there who have been arrested for crimes against the state."

After several days of travel, you spy the wall. Hundreds of men scurry about like insects as they labor.

As you get closer, you see the wall is made of dirt, reeds, and stones. Poles of bamboo are tied together to hold the muck of the wall in place. Some workers collect soil and rock and run it up the ladders in woven baskets. You watch others use heavy tools to pound the earth down into place.

Off and on, construction of the Great Wall of China lasted for 1,700 years.

Turn the page.

The height of the wall is more than 12 feet. The top is wide enough for several men to walk side by side.

Your father goes to speak with a group of soldiers overseeing the project. You take a closer look at the newly built section of the wall. You are surprised to see your boyhood teacher working as a common laborer. Should you talk to him?

To speak with your teacher, turn to page **34.**

To ignore him, turn to page **35.**

To see the building of the Great Wall would be exciting, but you don't want to fall behind on your lessons. "Your hesitation tells me your decision is already made," Qi Kong says. "We shall view it together in the future."

On your way to school, a familiar voice calls out. "Come! I want to show you something!" your friend Ban Lun says as he greets you with a friendly wave.

"What is it?"

"Not here. At home, in my father's study."

"What about school?"

"This is bigger than a day of school."

➤To go with Lun to learn his secret, turn to page 25.

➤To continue on to school by yourself, turn to page 38.

At last you may have a chance to see the books you have yearned to read! You can hardly wait for the day to end. You race home to quickly eat, and then return to the library garden.

From the shadows comes a voice: "You are the one who desires forbidden knowledge?" You nod. "You realize you are going against the direct rule of the emperor, yes?"

"I love my emperor, but I also want to know of China's past and the teachings of the great masters. Surely a book cannot be so dangerous that the emperor should fear a humble student reading it."

The figure steps out of the shadows. He is a member of Emperor Qin's Imperial Court! "Follow me," he says.

➻ *To follow the mysterious figure, turn to page* **31**.

➻ *To refuse to go, turn to page* **33**.

If Lun is willing to miss school, it must be important. You follow him down the many narrow streets to his home.

"So what's the big secret?" you finally ask. Reaching behind a shelf, Lun removes a scroll, a book made of a long bolt of silk wrapped around a wooden rod. Wordlessly, he hands the book to you. Your best friend has just handed you a copy of the *Analects*!

"Where did you get this?" you whisper as you unfurl the delicate silk.

"My father hid this copy when the emperor decided to destroy all books about Confucius," Lun replies. "But I'm afraid my family will get in trouble if it's discovered here."

Turn the page.

The *Analects* is a collection of conversations with Confucius recorded by his students around 500 BC.

You are the son of one of the emperor's greatest generals. Your loyalties are to your father and the throne. You know the punishment for owning this text may be death.

Lun looks at you with wide eyes. "You won't tell anyone, will you?"

➤ To keep the book a secret, go to page **27**.

➤ To reveal the presence of the book to authorities, turn to page **40**.

26

You hold the silken scroll in your hands. You want to help your friend, and you also want to read the book.

"I will hide the book," you announce, slipping it in the folds of your robe.

"You?" Lun says in surprise.

"My father is away to oversee construction of the Great Wall. This gives me time to find a hiding place. Words and ideas are not the danger here. Fear and misunderstanding are."

Lun frowns, not sure if he likes this idea. "What if the book is discovered?"

"Then I will take responsibility for my actions. But no one would suspect the son of a general to have an illegal document."

➤ To hide the book at home, turn to page 28.

➤ To keep the book in another place, turn to page 41.

As you step back out onto the street, you feel as if everyone is watching you. If you were to be discovered carrying the scroll of Confucius, how would you explain your actions to your father?

Stay calm, you tell yourself. Think like a soldier on a mission. You enter your house. Now to hide the book, but where?

"What is that, my son?" a familiar voice asks.

You turn to face your father, who stares at you with narrowed eyes. "Just a book, Father," you answer, trying to stay calm. "I thought you had left for the Great Wall."

"I came back to see if you would change your mind," he says, holding out a hand. "May I see what you are reading?"

You have no choice. You give your father the scroll. As he begins to read, his frowning face grows pale.

"You will not receive mercy from the emperor for owning this book just because you are my son," the general says.

Your father speaks the truth. You are sentenced to die on a cold, bleak morning. As you march alone to the scaffold to be hanged, you know you have forever shamed your family.

THE END

To follow another path, turn to page 13.
To read the conclusion, turn to page 103.

Although you are tempted to go to the meeting, you are still suspicious. You decide to show the note to your father.

"I am glad you brought this to me," he says. "Other learned men, as well as students such as yourself, have been tricked in this manner."

"What happened to them?"

Your father pauses. "Members of the emperor's inner circle helped set traps to discover who was loyal and who was not. But the emperor was merciful. Their punishment was to be sent to work building the Great Wall."

"I would not have gone to the meeting even if the note were true," you say.

Your father smiles. "I know, my son, I know."

THE END

To follow another path, turn to page 13.
To read the conclusion, turn to page 103.

"I know you! You are—"

He interrupts. "No names, please. After all, aren't we all merely humble students in search of knowledge?"

You relax. He seems sincere.

"Join me inside the library. However, I want to make sure you know what you are doing. You are taking a great risk to gain access to these scrolls. Do you understand?"

You take a deep breath. "I understand."

The two of you enter the library. However, what is inside is not forbidden books, but your own father, along with a second soldier.

"So it is true," your father says.

Turn the page.

"Father! I can explain!" you stammer, but it is too late.

"Take him," your father says. "He is no longer my son."

Weeks later, you find yourself banished and packing down soil while building the Great Wall. You are stripped of your honor, your education, and your family. You look out across the vibrant blue sky, but your soul is heavy. Because of your stubborn curiosity, you have lost everything you ever cared about.

THE END

To follow another path, turn to page 13.
To read the conclusion, turn to page 103.

You sense all is not as it seems. "Thank you for the opportunity, but I must say no," you say firmly.

The man smiles wolfishly. "A very wise decision. Word has reached the ears of the Imperial Court that the son of General Kong might be … untrustworthy."

"I can be trusted," you say, offended.

"So I see. But one who would go against the desires of the emperor could not be trusted."

You nod. "I understand."

"Then go, and be careful in the future." You leave the garden behind the library with a sense of relief. Knowing ancient secrets seems much less important now.

THE END

To follow another path, turn to page 13.
To read the conclusion, turn to page 103.

"Teacher Liu! What are you doing here?"
Your former teacher turns and stares at you with a sad expression.

"I displeased the emperor," he whispers. "I dared to speak and teach the forbidden words of the great Confucius and was arrested."

You had always wondered what happened to your teacher. Now that you know, you feel sad. How many other men of learning have suffered the same fate?

Suddenly the idea of becoming a soldier seems less appealing. You decide your life will be spent gathering knowledge. Tomorrow you will begin the journey back as a scholar. You have chosen your own path.

THE END

To follow another path, turn to page 13.
To read the conclusion, turn to page 103.

Slaves and prisoners worked day and night on the Great Wall.

Your former teacher looks over at your father and his soldiers with an expression of disgust. You sadly realize that the two of you have nothing to talk about. You approach another group of workers.

"Do you know how long the wall is?" you ask.

Turn the page.

An elderly man steps forward and shrugs. "Honorable sir, the wall is as long as it needs to be." He bows and returns to his work.

You ponder the man's statement. Is he making a joke at your expense, or is he serious? You notice that each part of the wall is being built in layers.

"Why not use something besides dirt to make this mighty wall?" you suggest.

"We use what we are given, and that is the earth," the man replies. "Once a section is complete, we move the bamboo frames over, and start again from the ground up. The process is slow, but the wall is strong."

You go back to your father's side. "What do you think?" the general asks you.

"I think my future is with you, in the army," you reply. "I want to help keep our country as safe as this wall." The general smiles proudly. You are a good and loyal son.

THE END

To follow another path, turn to page 13.
To read the conclusion, turn to page 103.

You arrive at school, only to see an official from the office of the emperor approach your teacher. When class begins, your teacher stands before the rest of you and speaks: "This morning, one of the forbidden texts was found in the home of your classmate Ban Lun."

Even though your mouth is almost too dry to speak, you raise your hand. "What will happen to him?"

Emperor Qin spared only a few books from destruction, including some on agriculture and medicine.

Your teacher's aged face is grim. "The entire family is to be executed."

You try to pay attention to the lesson that follows, but your mind stays on your friend—and your own possible fate. "What if I had gone with Lun?" you wonder. "Could I have stopped this, or would I have been arrested as well?"

Suddenly you lose any desire you still had to be a scholar. You know you made the right choice to become a soldier.

THE END

To follow another path, turn to page 13.
To read the conclusion, turn to page 103.

You hold the scroll in your hands. "Even though I do not agree with the laws, I am still honor-bound to turn it over," you say.

"Then I have doomed my family!" Lun wails.

"Do you think I would put my best friend to death?" you say. "I must give it to the authorities. However, I do not need to say who owned it. I will say the scroll was misfiled and discovered during my research at the central library."

You leave the house with a heavy heart. To protect your friend, you must lie to your father. To obey the emperor, you must destroy a book filled with lessons that you would like to know. "The life of a solider is a life of duty," you say sadly.

THE END

To follow another path, turn to page 13.
To read the conclusion, turn to page 103.

40

You leave with the scroll, but are not sure where to hide such a precious item. Then you have an idea.

"I'm going to hide this in plain sight at the library," you murmur to yourself. "The older texts are rarely used. I can drop this behind a cabinet, and it will be just another lost book."

Mentally congratulating yourself on your cleverness, you begin to run. You want to hide the scroll as soon as possible.

"Halt!" a voice cries out. You turn around to see two soldiers approaching Lun's house.

Turn the page.

"Why are you running?" they ask.

"I'm going to the library. I am behind in my studies."

"Are you friends with him?" the solider asks, pointing up the walkway. You see a frightened Lun being led down the path by a third soldier.

"I am, but I do not understand."

"We have received word that a banned book was being kept in the house. What book are you carrying?"

You are arrested with Lun. The emperor sentences you both to work on the Great Wall for the rest of your lives.

You could have chosen to go with your father to oversee the building of the wall. Now you will be working on it as a prisoner.

While laborers worked on the wall, horsemen patrolled the area to keep invaders away.

✦ THE END

To follow another path, turn to page 13.
To read the conclusion, turn to page 103.

Girls were mainly taught housekeeping skills, but some also learned to read and write.

CHAPTER 3

The Female Emperor of China

In the midst of the Tang Dynasty, the first female emperor, Wu Zetian, came into power. Under her rule, many positive changes have taken place in China. The empress has reduced the farmers' taxes. She allows farmers to keep a fair share of their crops. With this prosperity, peace has come about in most of the country.

You are a 15-year-old girl living in the year 691. Your family lives in a small hut in a village near Mount Tai. Your father works as a farmer, providing China with much-needed food.

Turn the page.

You attend the local Buddhist temple to learn about the Buddha, a religious leader who practiced compassion. Your grandmother is teaching you to write, but most of your time is spent doing housework and weaving.

Early one morning, you wake up excited. "I can't wait for the Moon Festival tonight!" you tell your grandmother.

Each fall everyone in your village gathers for a celebration during the full moon. They eat moon cakes, drink ceremonial wine, and write poetry in honor of Chang Er, the goddess of the moon.

"I want to see Chang Er in the moon this year," you say.

"Well, right now I just want to see food in the pot," Grandmother snorts.

As you watch your grandmother tear bok choy into strips, you think about her hard life. You don't know if you want to stay a peasant forever. You wish for adventure.

"Grandmother, how did the empress get to be the first female ruler?"

Grandmother stirs the bok choy. "I can tell you, but please get more wood for the fire first."

You head outside, eager to get back to hear the story. Like other families in the village, your wood is stored in a small hut near the stream. You carefully make your way through the early morning darkness to the hut.

At the stream, you notice a smell of cooking meat. "Hello?" you ask in a nervous voice. "Who's there?"

➤To ignore the smell and return home, turn to page **48**.

➤To follow your nose, turn to page **51**.

Hearing no response in the woods, you return to the hut. "I have the wood, Grandmother. Will you tell me the story now?"

Grandmother begins her tale. "When I was younger, I worked at the Buddhist nunnery. After a time, a group of women from Emperor Taizong's court was sent to stay there."

You listen intently, unaware of this part of your grandmother's past.

"Emperor Taizong had died. All those in his court were supposed to live out their lives in prayer for his soul." Here, Grandmother stops and looks at you, her eyes linking you to that time. "In this group was a teenage girl. She had a dream of making her future bright on her own terms. This was young Wu."

You are surprised. How did the future empress go from being a nun to becoming the most powerful woman in China?

Empress Wu Zetian was also known as Wu Zhao.

Turn the page.

Grandmother continues. "Young Wu believed in herself enough to take advantage of any opportunity. Plus she had fallen in love with Gaozong, the emperor's son. A year after his father's death, Gaozong visited the nunnery and saw Wu. It was as if no time had passed since their last meeting. He married her and took her to his court, making Wu his consort. From there, she worked her way into the position of power."

As Grandmother finishes her story, you hear a sound outside and remember the strange smells you noticed as you were gathering wood. "Grandmother, I think someone is staying in the woods near the stream."

"Really?" Grandmother replies. "I wonder who it is?"

➤ To investigate in the woods, turn to page **58**.

➤ To stay at home and prepare for the Moon Festival, turn to page **60**.

As you investigate, you discover a young man cooking his breakfast. The man's clothes are torn and dirty, and he is covered in dirt and scratches.

You approach in friendship. He warily eyes you as you draw nearer. "Nihao," you say, bowing in greeting.

The man pauses and replies, "Hello to you as well."

"Where are you headed?" you ask.

"I'm not sure," he replies "I am Shao. My family lives in Chou. I was an official in Her Majesty's Imperial Court. I discovered some officials were stealing money from the farmers in my district. I reported them to the empress. The men denied their wrongdoing and said I was the thief. Now they are trying to kill me."

Turn the page.

"What will you do?" you ask, alarmed.

"That is what I am trying to decide. If Her Majesty herself can't protect me, then maybe I should leave China."

You think for a few seconds. "Perhaps my family can help you."

Shao looks hopeful, but then sighs. "I don't want to put them in any danger," he says.

➻To insist on Shao returning with you,
go to page **53**.

➻To leave Shao in the woods, turn to **55**.

"Shao, you must come with me. We can hide you until tonight, if that will help."

The man considers your idea. He agrees to go to your hut.

"Father, Mother, Grandmother, this is Shao," you say. "He needs our help."

Your father rises and bows. Shao returns the gesture. The visitor acknowledges Grandmother and Mother. He sits next to you and tells his story. There is silence around the table. Even your little sister, Jo, is quiet.

Finally Father speaks. "I do not know who these men are who are chasing you. But I do know that running from your problems will never solve anything. My advice is to return and face your accusers."

Turn the page.

Shao shakes his head. "I would never make it. To even try is my death sentence."

"Not if you go out boldly. Perhaps my daughter and my mother could accompany you to court. We can say you are their guard. No one will try and hold back an escort for two women traveling to meet with the empress."

Shao ponders the plan. "I do not know. It is still risky."

Father nods in agreement. "If you are going, you should go right away." He turns to you and Grandmother and asks what you would like to do. It would be an amazing opportunity to meet the empress, but you hate the thought of missing the festival.

➨To go to court with Grandmother and Shao, turn to page **56**.

➨To stay and attend the Moon Festival, turn to page **65**.

"You're right. I don't want to put my family in danger, either," you tell Shao. You wish the traveler luck and leave him in the woods.

You gather up the wood Grandmother had requested. But before you can make your way back, two men appear. They are wearing the colors of the court of the empress.

"We seek an enemy of the state," one of the men says. "We suspect he is hiding in this forest."

The second man nods toward the armload of kindling you carry. "While you collected your wood, did you see or hear anything out of the ordinary?"

➦To respond truthfully, turn to page **62**.

➦To lie to protect Shao, turn to page **64**.

You, Grandmother, and Shao set out for the court of the empress. You have packs on your backs for the journey. Shao has bathed and carries himself like a true nobleman. Over the many days of travel, you learn that Shao is a merchant's son. He has traveled the Silk Road as a trader and has even been to the Great Wall.

"I would love to have such adventures," you tell him.

Weeks later you get to the court. Shao brings his case to the empress. She is beautiful and frightening at the same time, with her large headdress and commanding voice. When she learns why Shao fled the court, there is no hesitation. She orders that Shao's accusers be put to death.

Her Majesty takes notice of you. She offers you the opportunity to stay and become a lady-in-waiting. Your Grandmother may stay as your guardian. Your duties would include acting as the empress' secretary and companion.

Empress Wu encouraged women to become educated and participate in politics.

→To accept the offer from the empress, turn to page **68**.

→To return home, turn to page **70**.

You go back outside and head for the stream, but then you hear men's voices. You crouch low to stay hidden. You see three men—two of them dressed in the armor of the empress' army, and a third man wearing humble clothing. His face is bleeding from several wounds.

"Please don't do this," he says. "I am innocent, I tell you!" His pleas are ignored, and with a swipe of a sharp blade, his throat is cut.

You gasp in shock. You hope the men didn't hear you.

"A fitting end for someone who betrayed the trust of the empress," the soldier says as he puts away his weapon. They drop the man's body by the stream and stride away, leaving him on the cold ground.

You slowly approach the dying man. "Is there anything I can for do?" you ask softly.

"My name is Shao," he whispers. "I am an honorable man. Please say a prayer for me."

"Of course," you reply. "Is there anything else?"

Shao is silent. He is dead.

You sit beside him and look to the sky, knowing you will never forget the cruelty you witnessed or the name of the man who died at your side. Was he really guilty of betraying the empress? You'll never know.

THE END

To follow another path, turn to page 13.
To read the conclusion, turn to page 103.

"Perhaps it was my imagination," you say.

Grandmother asks if you have the moon cakes ready for tonight's festival.

"I do!" you say proudly. You unwrap a small package, revealing two delicious-looking cakes. Each is about the size of your hand and will be cut into quarters to be shared at the ceremony.

"I filled them with lotus seed paste, just like you taught me," you tell Grandmother. "I also baked four egg yolks in the middle to represent the four phases of the moon."

"Good," Grandmother says. Your cheeks flush at her praise of your baking.

You look out the window and wish the morning sun would hurry and set, so the full moon would appear. But for now, you will work and wait. Tonight will be here soon enough.

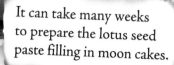

It can take many weeks to prepare the lotus seed paste filling in moon cakes.

THE END

To follow another path, turn to page 13.
To read the conclusion, turn to page 103.

"I … I did see a stranger today."

"His name is Shao, and he is a dangerous man," says one of the soldiers.

"Dangerous?" you ask. Shao did not appear to be a threat. He looked tired and weary, but not a danger to anyone.

"He once was a member of the court of the empress. He became greedy, and tried to take more than he was allowed. He has killed good men to protect his riches, and now he is on the run."

"What will happen to him?"

"That is up to the empress to decide. However, she is a fair and just woman. I am sure he will be treated honorably."

You give them directions and watch them go. You almost follow, but stop. You do not want to see Shao captured. You suspect he is going to be executed, but you had to do the right thing to protect your family.

THE END

To follow another path, turn to page 13.
To read the conclusion, turn to page 103.

You think about Shao. You believe his story and in his innocence. "No," you say. "I have seen no one."

"Are you sure?" the lead soldier says. "Lying could be very bad for you and your family."

"I am sorry, but I have not seen another person today in these woods."

The men nod curtly and continue on their way.

"Poor Shao," you think, glad you have kept his secret. You can only hope he is able to escape these two pursuers and prove his innocence. And you can only pray the soldiers don't find out you lied.

THE END

To follow another path, turn to page 13.
To read the conclusion, turn to page 103.

"I don't want to miss this year's Moon Festival. I want to write a poem for Chang Er," you say.

"I've seen many moons. You should stay and I will go," Grandmother replies. "This is probably my last chance for a great adventure."

That night your grandmother and Shao leave on their journey. The rest of your family and the other villagers trek up Mount Tai. Overhead, the moon is full and bright.

Turn the page.

Your father clears his throat, and speaks. "This is the legend of Chang Er flying to the moon. Once there was a great warrior called Hou Yi. He married a beautiful girl named Chang Er. Soon after, he met the Heavenly Queen Mother, who gave him a bottle filled with the Elixir of Immortality. One night, Chang Er was attacked by an evil man who wanted the elixir. Rather than give it to him, she drank it herself and flew into the air. She landed on the moon, and for every night since has watched over her husband to keep him safe."

You watch as the group eats their moon cakes, and you bite into your own. Then inspiration strikes. You have a scroll and your pen and ink. You sit under the light of the moon and scratch out a few lines of poetry.

It is breaking, this pale light over us

Shards of love, falling cleanly

What was cold is warm

The night leaps up, awake!

We are joined as one.

Forever.

You feel content and happy. You may never be as rich or educated as the empress. You might not have exciting adventures. But you will write beautiful poems about your simple life. Maybe that is your destiny.

67

THE END

To follow another path, turn to page 13.
To read the conclusion, turn to page 103.

You accept the offer. But it comes with a price. While your grandmother may stay, you will not be able to send for the rest of your family. You may visit them, but your time will be limited. Your life is now all about pleasing the empress.

Years later, you have progressed in the court. The empress has encouraged your intelligence and drive. You receive an education and become a poet. You are sad when your grandmother dies, but soon you marry the nobleman who first brought you to the court—Shao. You begin a family of your own.

Your children beg you to tell your story over and over. Each time you speak the words, you can hardly believe what has happened to you. Though you often miss your parents, your life is rich and full. You have achieved your destiny.

Brides in ancient China traditionally wore red on their wedding day.

THE END

To follow another path, turn to page 13.
To read the conclusion, turn to page 103.

The empress waits for your answer.

"Empress," you say softly. "Your offer is generous and kind, but I must refuse."

"Why is that, child?" Empress Wu asks sharply. You get the feeling she is not used to having her generosity turned down.

"I am still young, and I love my family. I do not wish to leave them or my village. I thought I wanted adventure, but now I see what riches I already have at home."

The empress smiles, and her face softens. "I see. Then return to your village. But know that if you are ever in need of anything, you may send word to me."

You bow, honored by her words. Perhaps in the future you can return and serve the empress in another role. But for now, your rightful place is in your simple little hut.

THE END

To follow another path, turn to page 13.
To read the conclusion, turn to page 103.

The Silk Road was full of travelers on their way to make trades and purchases.

CHAPTER 4

Danger in Dunhuang

You breathe the air deeply in your lungs. The scent of the city of Dunhuang is a mix of spices, animals, and sweat. "Smells like adventure!" you think to yourself.

The year is 1420. Dunhuang is located at the western end of the Gansu Corridor, between two major trade routes. This makes it a popular stop for traders throughout China and central Asia.

You look around the busy streets. You traveled with a small caravan to reach this point, but now you are alone. You try to calm the butterflies in your stomach.

Turn the page.

You are the 17-year-old son of a silk merchant. Normally you travel with your father on the famed Silk Road along the northwestern border of China. But this time you are on your own. You have been entrusted with a great duty. You are here to make an important trade on behalf of Emperor Ming Chengzu.

On the back of your camel are many bolts of the finest silk found in China. Your parents wove the silks at your home in Hangzhou. As a little boy, you cared for the caterpillars that spun their silken cocoons. Each day you tended to the silkworms by feeding them mulberry leaves. You watched intently as your father dipped the cocoons in hot water. Soon the delicate creations would unravel, revealing a single long strand of silk.

With such precious silk in your pack, you had better keep moving. Many thieves are known to patrol Dunhuang in hopes of robbing an unwary traveler. You nudge your camel to move ahead.

➻To explore the city some more, turn to page 76.

➻To continue on your mission, turn to page 80.

You decide to explore Dunhuang. You ride up to a booth run by a young woman about your age. The girl's mother watches you carefully.

"So," you say in your most charming voice. "Other than the visions inside this tent, where is the most beautiful part of this city?"

She laughs musically. "The Mogao cave temples are where the Buddhist monks meditated and prayed for years. The artwork is breathtaking."

The Mogao caves are some distance from the city, along the Silk Road. You remember your father's words: "Only a fool travels the Silk Road alone." For a small fee, you hire a guard on horseback to accompany you.

After a few hours' travel, you arrive at the entrance to the caves. You leave your camel with the guard and enter. Once inside, you marvel at the sculptures and paintings. The caves are mostly rectangular, with plastered ceilings covered with dazzling paintings. There are more than 200 caves to explore, all with statues and artwork.

You are in awe of the beauty, and time quickly passes. Soon you realize you have been wandering in the caves for hours.

➤*To explore more of the caves, turn to page **78**.*

➤*To return to Dunhuang to complete your mission, turn to page **86**.*

You decide to spend a bit more time in the caves. Who knows if you'll ever have the chance to visit again?

"There are hundreds of these caves, you know," a voice says.

You turn to see the calm face of a boy about your age. "I guess I won't be able to enjoy them all today, then," you say.

The other boy laughs. "I should think not. I have been coming here for years and still haven't seen them all. I am Bao."

You introduce yourself. Then Bao explains, "According to legend, a Buddhist monk named Le Zun had a vision. He saw a thousand Buddhas in a dream, and this inspired him to start the Mogao caves."

The Mogao caves in Dunhuang are also known as the Caves of a Thousand Buddhas.

The two of you step into another cavern and look at some of the sculptures dedicated to the Buddha. You suddenly yawn and stretch. Your day is beginning to catch up with you. The time has come to get back to work.

"Thank you for the information, but now I must return to Dunhuang," you say.

"Surely another hour won't hurt, will it?" asks Bao.

→To return to Dunhuang, turn to page **98**.

→To stay in the caves with Bao, turn to page **99**.

You have come to Dunhuang to trade your silk for a special sculpture known as the Jade Dragon. The owner of the statue wants silk of the highest quality, and that is what your family makes. A successful trade will mean great reward. But failure could lead to personal shame and possibly death if the emperor is not pleased.

You ride your camel up the main street of the marketplace. Vendors dot nearly every foot of space as crowds shuffle from one stand to another. You stop and hire a guard on horseback to protect you.

You spy the jade merchant's tent. The tent's color is deep green like the jade gemstone itself. Your guard waits outside the tent as you enter.

"Greetings," the merchant begins. "I see you have silk as your load. Do you wish to trade? I am Chien, at your service." He bows deeply.

You bow in return. "I am the son of Po Huang."

Chien laughs merrily. "I know your father and his amazing skills with silk."

"Then you also know I am here to receive an item for His Majesty."

Chien snaps his fingers, and soon one of his men places the heavy jade sculpture in your hands. You remove your bolts of silk for Chien. A cascade of vibrant color flows as each bolt unfurls.

Turn the page.

"Your family's silk is the finest I've seen," Chien remarks, as his assistant carries the fabric bolts away. "Now that our deal is done, you should give yourself some time to reflect and relax. Perhaps you would like to visit the beautiful Mogao caves."

Silkworm cocoons were placed on racks. After being heated, the silk thread of each cocoon was unraveled.

→To explore the caves, go to page **83**.

→To sell the rest of your silk and then return home, turn to page **92**.

You leave Chien with your guard close behind and go to the caves. The Jade Dragon is too heavy to carry, so you secure it in one of the bags on your camel.

"I will return before nightfall," you tell your guard. "Stay alert, and I shall pay you double once I no longer need your protection."

While admiring the art and sculpture in the caves, you meet a young Buddhist monk who is deep in meditation. However, he is friendly and invites you to sit. He introduces himself as Xuanzang. "Tell me about yourself," he says. "Why have you traveled here?"

Turn the page.

You tell him about your mission to bring back the Jade Dragon for the emperor. You share your worries and fears. "What happens if I fail in my task?" you ask.

"Fail or not fail. The choice, my son, is to do the best you possibly can."

Upon leaving the caves, you look around for the guard and your camel. They are nowhere to be found. You walk a little farther and see an old woman. You ask her if she has seen a guard on horseback and a camel.

"I saw a man on horseback leading a camel toward the city."

You try to swallow the fear rising in your throat. "H-how long ago?"

Creating jade sculptures was difficult work. After being carved and engraved, the jade required much polishing.

"About an hour ago. He appeared to be in a hurry."

The guard has stolen the Jade Dragon! You'll never catch him now. And all you have is the purse of coins you're carrying. What are you going to do?

➻To stay in Dunhuang and avoid being shamed at home, turn to page **89**.

➻To return home and face your punishment with honor, turn to page **90**.

As you prepare to head back to Dunhuang, you realize that you are hungry. You choose a restaurant. "I will be back shortly," you tell your guard, who is seated on his horse. "Do not let my camel out of your sight."

"As you wish," the guard replies.

You feel uneasy as you start to eat. Your intuition tells you to check on your camel. Your feelings were correct! You spy the "guard" leading your camel off. He is a thief!

In a flash, you catch up to the guard. The camel runs away as you drag the bandit off the horse's back.

Screaming at the top of your lungs, you cry, "Ni gan ma! What are you doing?"

The man scrambles to his feet, holding up his hands and backing away.

A young boy in ragged clothing walks the camel back to you. "Where are you from?" he asks.

"I am from Hangzhou. I am on a mission for the emperor. I am heading for the jade merchant," you say. "Thank you for bringing back my camel."

Feeling exhausted, you decide that tomorrow will be soon enough to complete your job for the emperor. The boy, whose name is Micho, invites you to his family's home. It is a small house for a family of five, but everyone is kind. They offer you tea with your meal. Dinner and conversation are pleasant, and you enjoy yourself.

Turn the page.

That night you are just beginning to fall asleep on your mat next to Micho and his older brother. But you jolt awake when you hear a camel crying out and some men whispering. Could your guard have returned with other thieves to try to rob you again?

→To wake up Micho, turn to page 94.

→To go outside, turn to page 96.

While your honor is tarnished, the future is yours to choose. As you make the long walk back across the hot desert sands to Dunhuang, you come up with a plan.

Why return home in disgrace? If you do not return, everyone will assume you perished on the Silk Road. There is no dishonor in beginning a new life if the old one is now dead to you.

"First, I will need a new name," you whisper. "And while I have no silks to trade, I do have my skills and money in my pocket. I can start my own silk business." As you enter the city, you look out at the throng of people. You hope you have made the right choice.

THE END

To follow another path, turn to page 13.
To read the conclusion, turn to page 103.

You walk back to the city and buy a donkey. It's going to be a long journey home. You don't look forward to your father's anger or the emperor's wrath.

You reflect on the words of the Buddha, who says the great heart of compassion can be found in all beings. It is hard to feel compassion for one who has stolen your livelihood. You hope, after you arrive home weeks later, that your father remembers the Buddha's teachings and that he spares your hide.

But when you return empty-handed, your father is enraged. "You have shamed the family! You are no son of mine."

With that, he kicks you out of the house. You are stained with failure, and the emperor still does not have his Jade Dragon.

Soon you are summoned to the court to explain your failure. The emperor's advisers don't believe your story of being robbed. You are a disgrace, your family is dishonored, and you are sentenced to death.

Emperor Ming Chengzu was also known as the Yongle Emperor.

THE END

To follow another path, turn to page 13.
To read the conclusion, turn to page 103.

You spend the rest of the afternoon selling silk, getting fine prices for your family's work. You now have money and have completed your task.

After several weeks of travel, you arrive home. You present the Jade Dragon to your father. He in turn gives it to Emperor Ming Chengzu, ensuring a happy ending for everyone. Riches rain down upon your family. The emperor himself compliments you on your successful mission.

"I could use a brave man with a quick mind such as yours in my court," the emperor says. "Are you planning on staying in the silk trade?"

"Well, I had hoped to take the Imperial examination so I could have a job working for the government. This would secure my future, and allow me to serve your court," you say. "But I have no sponsor to support my plans."

"You do now," the emperor replies. "I will provide a sponsor as an extra gift for your fine service."

You study hard. You learn about history, literature, philosophy, and ethics. You pass the examination. You become an educated member of the government. Your dreams have all come true.

93

THE END

To follow another path, turn to page 13.
To read the conclusion, turn to page 103.

"Micho! Wake up!" you whisper.

Micho opens his eyes and sees you rise from your mat. "What is wrong?" he asks.

"Do you hear those noises outside?"

Micho listens. "Yes," he says, "but do not go outside, my friend."

"Why?" you whisper back.

"You are very brave. But the odds are not in your favor. To fight a single thief in the light of day is one thing," Micho says. "Facing a group in the dark of night is another."

You curse yourself for your laziness. This wouldn't be happening if only you had taken the time to unpack the precious cargo carried by your camel.

"If my camel is taken, I lose all of my silk! What then?"

"Better to lose your silks than to lose your life," Micho replies. You decide your young friend is right. But you still might lose your life once you return home. With no silk, the emperor will not get his trade. If only you had finished the job today! Now you must throw yourself on His Majesty's mercy rather than challenge a band of thieves.

Tomorrow you will begin the long journey home empty-handed and in disgrace. You hope that the emperor's punishment isn't worse than confronting the thieves would have been.

THE END

To follow another path, turn to page 13.
To read the conclusion, turn to page 103.

95

Jumping up, you hop over the sleeping family, careful not to step on anyone. Out in the night air, your eyes adjust quickly to the dark. You spy your stolen camel. You chase the thieves, who are pulling the beast through the empty streets.

Buildings, tents, and fountains rush past as you focus on your task. Suddenly the thieves take a sharp turn, running out of the city and into the desert. They quickly outpace you as you struggle to follow.

The Takla Makan Desert is one of the largest sandy deserts in the world.

You refuse to give up. You run for what seems like hours. You no longer know the direction you're going. All you know is that this is the Takla Makan Desert. And the men are nowhere in sight.

You sink to the ground. The cool sand feels good on your sweaty skin. You fall into a restless sleep, feeling hopeless and exhausted.

The next day the sun burns your face. Thirst makes your mouth as dry and gritty as the sand dunes around you. All you can think of is finding water. But you are unable to trace your steps back to the city or find a water source in the desert. Within days you die, alone. Your body is swallowed up by the shifting sands, never to be seen again.

THE END

To follow another path, turn to page 13.
To read the conclusion, turn to page 103.

You say goodbye and turn from Bao to leave the caves. This is the last thing you remember before being hit from behind.

You fall to the hard cave ground, unconscious.

Later you awaken with a throbbing pain at the base of your skull. You check your pockets. Empty! Your so-called friend Bao has robbed you! Once you make your way out of the cave, you find your guard and your camel also missing.

No money, no camel, no silk, no future. You sigh deeply and resign yourself to the long walk back to Dunhuang. Your father will be furious, and what about the emperor? Your shoulders slump. Your adventure has ended before even beginning.

THE END

To follow another path, turn to page 13.
To read the conclusion, turn to page 103.

"Another hour, then," you say. "Especially since I have a guide."

Bao laughs and lights a torch. "I'm no expert, but I can show you caves visitors often miss."

You fall in step behind your new friend as the two of you wind your way deeper into the caverns. As time passes, you notice that the paintings and sculptures are becoming fewer. You also note that other people are nowhere to be found.

"Um, Bao?" you ask, becoming nervous at being alone with a person you just met.

"Yes?"

"How much farther?"

Turn the page.

The murals painted by Buddhist monks in the Mogao caves include portaits and paintings from religious stories.

Bao turns and pulls out a knife. "This should be far enough. Your money, please. And don't bother yelling for help. No one can hear you."

Your face grows hot with shame as you hand over your coins. "Do not follow me," Bao orders.

You watch as the light of the torch grows faint. Darkness surrounds you. You try to step forward but trip over a large stone. You land hard on your back, breaking your neck in the fall. You lie there on the ground, looking up into the blackness. You are alone and unable to move. Lost in these caves without light, water, or help, you will be dead in a few days.

THE END

To follow another path, turn to page 13.
To read the conclusion, turn to page 103.

Marco Polo was one of the first Europeans to travel the Silk Road.

CHAPTER 5

China's Past, Present, and Future

The rich culture of ancient China caused the legendary explorer Marco Polo to describe it as "a land of wonders." Instead of focusing on conquering their neighbors, the Chinese people focused on art, science, and technology.

The Chinese created fireworks, gunpowder, and the mechanical crossbow. Many experts believe they built the first cannons as well. The Chinese invented the wheelbarrow, which they called a "wooden ox." They used a waterwheel to power the first clocks. They discovered magnetism and made the first compass. The Chinese are also credited with the first kites, the umbrella, the rudder used for steering ships, matches, the game of chess, and even an early earthquake detector.

One of the ancient Chinese people's greatest achievements was the Great Wall, parts of which still stand. The building of the wall spanned several dynasties and helped to protect the country from invaders from the north. Today the wall is seen as one of the major architectural accomplishments of mankind.

The Qin Dynasty succeeded in adopting one written language for the entire country. Roads were built across the country, making it easier to travel and trade. Canals were introduced. One kind of money was created.

During the Ming Dynasty, the arts reached new heights. Painters created landscapes on silk and paper. Other craftsmen made beautiful sculptures, jewelry, porcelain dishes, and textiles. Literature and poetry became popular, and many of the poets of this era are still read today.

Modern-day China is one of the world's leading producers of nearly any product one can imagine. This manufacturing boom has led China to establish business relationships across the globe.

The influence of the West can be seen in China's cars, furniture, and even entertainment. But the customs of ancient China remain in place and still govern the people's everyday lives.

For example, Confucianism is still important in China. Though forbidden during the Qin Dynasty, Confucianism was a leading philosophy of Chinese people for 2,000 years. Even today, millions continue to follow Confucius' teachings, which are based on manners, respect, and personal responsibility. In China, the past is as honored as the present.

Timeline

2100 BC—Some historians believe the era of ancient China begins.

600 BC—Laozi founds Taoism.

551 BC—Chinese teacher and philosopher Confucius is born.

479 BC—Confucius dies.

259 BC—First Emperor of China, Qin Shi Huangdi, is born.

221 BC—The Qin Dynasty begins.

220 BC—Construction begins on the Great Wall of China.

213 BC—Many books are destroyed by order of the emperor, including the *Analects*, which contains the teachings of Confucius.

210 BC—Qin Shi Huangdi dies.

206 BC—The Han Dynasty begins.

136 BC—Emperor Wu Di makes Confucianism the basis for government and official ideology.

AD 105—Paper is invented by the Chinese.

618—The Tang Dynasty begins.

690—Wu Zetian becomes the first and only female emperor to rule China.

850—The Chinese invention of gunpowder changes warfare.

906—The Tang Dynasty ends.

1368—The Ming Dynasty begins; work starts on extending and rebuilding the Great Wall with brick.

1402—Ming Chengzu, considered one of the greatest of all emperors, rules until 1424.

1644—The Ming Dynasty ends; construction stops on the Great Wall.

1911—The Qing Dynasty, the last imperial dynasty of China, ends.

Other Paths
to Explore

In this book you've seen three different perspectives and experiences of people living in ancient China. Perspectives on history are as varied as the people who lived it. Seeing history from many points of view is an important part of understanding it.

Here are some ideas for other points of view to explore:

+ Imagine that you lived in a time or place where most books were not allowed, such as during the Qin Dynasty. Would you be willing to risk your life to read books you believe you should be allowed to read?

+ The Great Wall of China is considered to be one of the Seven Wonders of the Ancient World. If you had the choice, would you rather help build the Great Wall or the Great Pyramid in Egypt?

+ Imagine you are an inventor in ancient China. Would you prefer to investigate new medicines for diseases such as malaria or study astronomy and events such as lunar eclipses?

READ MORE

Catel, Patrick. *What Did the Ancient Chinese Do for Me?* Chicago: Heinemann Library, 2011.

Deady, Kathleen W., and Muriel L. Dubois. *Ancient China: Beyond the Great Wall.* Mankato, Minn.: Capstone Press, 2012.

Friedman, Mel. *Ancient China.* New York: Children's Press, 2010.

Van Pelt, Todd, and Rupert Matthews. *Ancient Chinese Civilization.* New York: Rosen Central, 2010.

INTERNET SITES

Use FactHound to find Internet sites related to this book. All of the sites on FactHound have been researched by our staff.

Here's all you do:
Visit *www.facthound.com*
Type in this code: 9781429647786

Glossary

ban (BAN)—to forbid or make something illegal

bolt (BOLT)—a roll of something, such as cloth

compassion (kuhn-PASH-uhn)—concern for someone in trouble that leads to the desire to help that person

consort (KAHN-sort)—a husband or wife

destiny (DES-tih-nee)—a special purpose

dynasty (DYE-nuh-stee)—a period of time during which a country's rulers all come from one family

ethics (ETH-iks)—standards of behavior and moral judgment

imperial (im-PEER-ee-uhl)—relating to an empire or emperor

lotus (LOW-tuhs)—a water plant with large flowers;

monk (MUHNGK)—a man who lives in a religious community and promises to devote his life to his religion

mural (MYU-ruhl)—a painting on a wall

philosophy (fuh-LOSS-uh-fee)—the study of truth and knowledge

prosperity (prahs-PAYR-uh-tee)—doing very well or being a success

BIBLIOGRAPHY

Brook, Timothy. "The Merchant Network in 16th Century China: A Discussion and Translation of Zhang Han's 'On Merchants.' " *Journal of the Economic and Social History of the Orient* 24 (1981): 165–214.

Chang, Chun-shu. *The Rise of the Chinese Empire: Nation, State, and Imperialism in Early China, ca. 1600 B.C.–A.D. 8*. Ann Arbor: University of Michigan Press, 2007.

ChinaCulture.org. 10 April 2012. www.chinaculture.org

China History Forum. 10 April 2012. www.chinahistoryforum.com

Grotenhuis, Elizabeth Ten. "Stories of Silk and Paper." *World Literature Today* 80.4 (2006): 10–12.

Huang, Youqin, Gregory Veeck, Clifton W. Pannell, and Christopher J. Smith. *China's Geography: Globalization and the Dynamics of Political, Economic, and Social Change*. New York: Rowman & Littlefield Publishers, Lanham, Md.: 2006.

Simpson, Judith. *Ancient China*. Alexandria, Va.: Time-Life Books, 1996.

Women in World History. 10 April 2012. www.womeninworldhistory.com

INDEX